# Conference of the North American Chapter of the Association for Computational Linguistics: Human Language Technologies (NAACL HLT 2018)

## Tutorial Abstracts



New Orleans, Louisiana, USA
1 – 6 June 2018

ISBN: 978-1-5108-6351-4

**Printed from e-media with permission by:**

Curran Associates, Inc.
57 Morehouse Lane
Red Hook, NY 12571

**Some format issues inherent in the e-media version may also appear in this print version.**



Printed by Curran Associates, Inc. (2018)



Association for Computational Linguistics
209 N. Eighth Street
Stroudsburg, Pennsylvania 18360

Phone: 1-570-476-8006
Fax: 1-570-476-0860

acl@aclweb.org

**Additional copies of this publication are available from:**

Curran Associates, Inc.
57 Morehouse Lane
Red Hook, NY 12571 USA
Phone: 845-758-0400
Fax: 845-758-2633
Email: curran@proceedings.com
Web: www.proceedings.com

NAACL HLT 2018

# The 2018 Conference of the North American Chapter of the Association for Computational Linguistics: Human Language Technologies

## Tutorial Abstracts

June 1 2018
New Orleans, Louisiana

# Introduction

Welcome to the Tutorials Session of NAACL HLT 2018 in New Orleans.

The NAACL-HLT tutorials session is an opportunity for conference attendees to participate in a tutorial on a timely topic of importance to the field, and to hear from experts on that topic. This year, the tutorials committee comprised of tutorials chairs from four conferences: ACL, COLING, EMNLP and NAACL-HLT. A total of 51 tutorial submissions were received, of which 6 were selected for presentation at NAACL-HLT.

We hope you find the six NAACL-HLT tutorials for this year to combine depth within each tutorial, and breadth across a set of topics that demonstrate the increasing relevance of NLP to a wide range of fields within and beyond computer science.

We would like to thank Marilyn Walker (NAACL general chair), Ying Lin (NAACL website chair), Stephanie Lukin and Margaret Mitchell (NAACL publications chairs), and Priscilla Rasmussen (local arrangement chair) for their help during the whole process. We also want to extend our sincere gratitude to the other conferences' tutorial chairs who jointly helped with reviewing for all the tutorial submissions: Yoav Artzi, Jacob Eisenstein, Pascale Fung, Donia Scott, Marilyn Walker, Mausam, and Lu Wang.

Enjoy the tutorials!
NAACL 2018 Tutorial Co-chairs
Mohit Bansal
Rebecca Passonneau

# NAACL HLT Organizers

**General Chair**

Marilyn Walker, University of California, Santa Cruz
Contact: naacl2018@googlegroups.com

**Program Co-Chairs**

Heng Ji, Rensselaer Polytechnic Institute
Amanda Stent, Bloomberg
Contact: naacl2018-program@googlegroups.com

**Tutorials Committee**

Mohit Bansal, University of North Carolina
Rebecca Passonneau, Pennsylvania State University
Contact: naacl2018-tutorial-chairs@googlegroups.com

# Table of Contents

# Conference Program

**Friday, June 1, 2018**

**Morning Session**

09:00–12:30 *Modelling Natural Language, Programs, and their Intersection*
Graham Neubig and Miltiadis Allamanis

09:00–12:30 *Deep Learning Approaches to Text Production*
Claire Gardent and Shashi Narayan

09:00–12:30 *Scalable Construction and Reasoning of Massive Knowledge Bases*
Xiang Ren, Nanyun Peng and William Yang Wang

**12:30–15:00** ***Lunch***

**Afternoon Session**

15:00–17:30 *The interplay between lexical resources and Natural Language Processing*
Jose Camacho-Collados, Luis Espinosa Anke and Mohammad Taher Pilehvar

15:00–17:30 *Socially Responsible NLP*
Yulia Tsvetkov, Vinodkumar Prabhakaran and Rob Voigt

15:00–17:30 *Deep Learning for Conversational AI*
Pei-Hao Su, Nikola Mrkšić, Iñigo Casanueva and Ivan Vulić

# Modelling Natural Language, Programs, and their Intersection

Graham Neubig (Carnegie Mellon University), **Miltiadis** Allamanis (Microsoft Research)

## Description

Just like natural language is a tool that humans use to communicate with each-other, programming languages are tools that humans use to communicate with computers. Because of the increasing need for programs and programming in our working and everyday lives, there are now massive amounts of source code being produced every day. As a result, it is ever more important for an ever increasing segment of the populace to be able to understand and create programs to do what they would like to do. However, programming is a specialized skill, IT education is hard-pressed to make up for this demand.

One key insight that can help us tackle this problem is that source code is *bimodal*. While one modality is targeted towards explicitly instructing the hardware on the actions to perform, the other is targeted towards the humans that need to read, understand, maintain and extend the code. Given that it is humans that are producing the software, the human-oriented modality is very strong and often takes the form of natural language: from natural language identifiers, such as variable and method names, to code comments and natural language documentation.

As a result, there is recently a burgeoning interest in research that connects natural language with the programming language artifacts. This research area has the potential to improve the efficiency and ease of programming by making connections to natural language, which is (in general) easier for humans to understand and communicate with, particularly humans who are not yet well-versed in programming. Some examples of relevant tasks include:

- **Automatic explanation of programs in natural language (code-to-language):** Highly connected with the task of grounded natural language generation in the NLP community, this is the task of generating natural language explanations for source code artifacts, which will allow them to be understood more easily.
- **Automatic generation of programs from natural language specifications (language-to-code):** Highly connected with the task of semantic parsing in the NLP community, this is the task of translating natural language into code that allows for grounded executable representations of natural language. This also encompasses natural language code search, which retrieves relevant code snippets based on natural language queries.
- **Modelling the natural language elements of source code:** As mentioned above, much of source code itself contains elements that are expressed in natural language (e.g. variable names and code comments), giving a form of grounded semantics to these aspects of code.
- **Analysis of communication in collaborative software development communities:** The process of developing software, particularly in multi-party projects, is a collaborative act, and as a result, provides a rich source of data for analysis of grounded communication in collaborative environments, which can then be used to improve productivity in these environments.



*Proceedings of NAACL-HLT 2018: Tutorial Abstracts*, pages 1–3
New Orleans, Louisiana, June 1, 2018. 

In this tutorial, we will focus on machine learning models of source code and natural language tailored to tackle these tasks. These methods have attracted wide interest not only in the NLP community, but also in software engineering and machine learning conferences, attesting to the interdisciplinary nature and broad impact of this research field. An overview of many of these methods can be found in co-proposer Allamanis' survey on the topic [1].

First, we will analyze the relationship between source code and natural language text. The similarities and differences between those types of languages drive the design of the machine learning models used for understanding and generating code and connecting it to natural language. Furthermore, despite the formal nature of programming languages, there is an abundance of natural language artifacts embedded within source code and vica-versa. We will discuss these artifacts, their special characteristics and how they relate with existing NLP research. We will also show some examples of how source code and source code repositories present an interesting type of grounding for natural language, particularly instructional or procedural language.

The remainder of the tutorial will cover specific recent methods that have been used to tackle each of the four tasks above. In doing so, we will stress a number of aspects of the presented methods:

1. Why the natural language artifacts occuring in each of the projects are interesting, and perhaps unique, compared to other sources of natural language data.
2. How to make connections between natural language artifacts and the corresponding code, and how these connections can be used to benefit each of the tasks.
3. Specific modelling techniques that have proven useful in these tasks, and how they may be fed back to other applications in mainstream NLP research.

Finally, we will close our tutorial by discussing open problems and challenges.

## Outline of Contents

We aim for a three-hour tutorial to cover a reasonable range of aspects of this area. Times are approximate, and will be adjusted somewhat as we refine the tutorial content.

**Part 1**

- Introduction (30 minutes)
  - Motivation for modelling source code and natural language
  - Where does language appear in code and vice-versa?
  - The similarities and differences between natural and programming languages.
- Data sources (10 minutes)
- Methods for mapping from code to natural language (40 minutes)

**Part 2**

- Methods for mapping from language to code (45 minutes)
- Modelling natural language aspects of source code (15 minutes)
- Modelling communicative aspects of software projects (15 minutes)
- Conclusion (5 minutes)
  - Where should I start?

## Names/Affiliations

**Graham Neubig** (gneubig@cs.cmu.edu, http://phontron.com) is an assistant professor at Carnegie Mellon University specializing in natural language processing and machine learning. One of his major research interests is models that link together natural language and code, including summarizing the intent of code in natural language, generating code from natural language, or discovering the correspondences between the two modalities. He has previously given well-attended tutorials at NLP conferences (EMNLP and YRSNLP) and the Lisbon Machine Learning Summer School, and has won a number of best papers (e.g. EMNLP2016 and EACL2017) and given invited talks, including an upcoming one on this topic at the AAAI Workshop on NLP for Software Engineering.

**Miltos Allamanis** (miallama@microsoft.com, https://miltos.allamanis.com) is a researcher at Microsoft Research, Cambridge, UK at the Deep Program Understanding project. He is researching applications of machine learning and natural language processing to software engineering and programming languages to create smart software engineering tools for developers. Miltos has published in both machine learning and software engineering conferences and is an author of a recent survey on machine learning for source code (https://ml4code.github.io). He received his PhD at the University of Edinburgh, UK advised by Dr. Charles Sutton.

## Bibliography

[1] Allamanis, Miltiadis, et al. "A Survey of Machine Learning for Big Code and Naturalness." *ACM Computing Surveys.* To appear (2018).

# Deep Learning Approaches to Text Production

Claire Gardent and Shashi Narayan

May 2, 2018

## 1 Content and Relevance

Text production is a key component of many NLP applications.

In data-driven approaches, it is used for instance, to generate dialogue turns from dialogue moves [Wen et al., 2015, Wen et al., 2016, Novikova et al., 2017], to verbalise the content of Knowledge bases [Gardent et al., 2017a, Gardent et al., 2017b] or to generate natural English sentences from rich linguistic representations, such as dependency trees [Belz et al., 2011, Mille et al., 2018] or Abstract Meaning Representations [May and Priyadarshi, 2017, Konstas et al., 2017, Song et al., ].

In text-driven methods on the other hand, text production is at work in sentence compression [Knight and Marcu, 2000, Cohn and Lapata, 2008, Filippova and Strube, 2008, Pitler, 2010, Filippova et al., 2015, Toutanova et al., 2016]; sentence fusion [McKeown et al., 2010, Filippova, 2010, Thadani and McKeown, 2013]; paraphrasing [Dras, 1999, Barzilay and McKeown, 2001, Bannard and Callison-Burch, 2005, Wubben et al., 2010, Narayan et al., 2016, Dong et al., 2017, Mallinson et al., 2017]; sentence (or text) simplification [Siddharthan et al., 2004, Zhu et al., 2010, Woodsend and Lapata, 2011, Wubben et al., 2012, Narayan and Gardent, 2014, Xu et al., 2015, Narayan and Gardent, 2016, Zhang and Lapata, 2017, Narayan et al., 2017], text summarisation [Wan, 2010, Nenkova and McKeown, 2011, Woodsend and Lapata, 2010, Rush et al., 2015, Cheng and Lapata, 2016, Nallapati et al., 2016, Chen et al., 2016, Tan and Wan, 2017, See et al., 2017, Nallapati et al., 2017, Paulus et al., 2017, Yasunaga et al., 2017, Narayan et al., 2018a, Narayan et al., 2018b, Pasunuru and Bansal, 2018, Celikyilmaz et al., 2018] and end-to-end dialogue systems [Li et al., 2017].

Following the success of encoder-decoder models in modeling sequence-rewriting tasks such as machine translation [Sutskever et al., 2011, Bahdanau et al., 2014], deep learning models have successfully been applied to the various text production tasks. For instance, [Rush et al., 2015] utilize a local attention-based model for abstractive summarisation, [Shang et al., 2015] propose an encoder-decoder model for response generation, [See et al., 2017] uses a hybrid of encoder-decoder model and pointer network [Vinyals et al., 2015] for story highlight generation, [Dong et al., 2017] exploits an encoder-decoder model for question rephrasing and [Konstas et al., 2017] for AMR generation.

In this tutorial, we will cover the fundamentals and the state-of-the-art research on neural models for text production. Each text production task raises a slightly different communication goal (e.g, how to take the dialogue context into account when producing a dialogue turn; how to detect and merge relevant information when summarising a text; or how to produce a well-formed text that correctly capture the information contained in some input data in the case of data-to-text generation). We will outline the constraints specific to each subtasks and examine how the existing neural models account for them.

## 2 Tutorial Outline

The tutorial will review deep learning approaches to text production. It will consider both text-to-text and data-to-text transformations. It aims to provide the audience with a good knowledge of text production systems, and a roadmap to get them started with the related work.



*Proceedings of NAACL-HLT 2018: Tutorial Abstracts*, pages 4–9
New Orleans, Louisiana, June 1, 2018. 

1. Introduction
   - Relevance of text production
   - Why deep learning for text production
2. Background
   - Deep learning basics
   - Generating Text using RNN LMs
3. Encoding Input Structure
   - Sequential encoders (Sentence compression, simplification, paraphrase generation and dialogue generation)
   - Hierarchical encoders (Document summarization)
   - Graph Encoders (Abstract Meaning Representations to text, structured data such as OWL, RDF and DB, to text)
4. Decoding and Semantic Adequacy
   - Attention and copy mechanism (accuracy)
   - Coverage mechanism (covering all the input)
5. Advanced Topics
   - Deep Reinforcement learning for text production
   - Convolutional Seq2Seq and Tranformer Models
6. Systems, Shared Tasks and Open Challenges

## 3 Presenters

**Claire Gardent**
Senior Research scientist
CNRS, LORIA, Nancy
`claire.gardent@loria.fr`
`https://members.loria.fr/CGardent/`

**Shashi Narayan**
Research Associate
School of Informatics, University of Edinburgh
`shashi.narayan@ed.ac.uk`
`http://homepages.inf.ed.ac.uk/snaraya2/`

Claire Gardent is a research scientist at CNRS (the French National Center for Scientific Research). Prior to joining the CNRS, she worked at the Université de Clermont-Ferrand, Saarbrücken Universität and Amsterdam Universiteit. She received her Ph.D. degree from the University of Edinburgh. Her research interests include (executable) semantic parsing, natural language generation and simplification and, more recently, the use of computational linguistics for linguistic analysis. She was nominated Chair of the EACL and acted as program chair for various international conferences, workshops and summer schools (EACL, ENLG, SemDIAL, SIGDIAL, ESSLLI, *SEM). She currently heads the WebNLG project (Nancy, Bolzano, Stanford SRI) and is the chair of SIGGEN, the ACL Special Interest Group in Natural Language Generation. Recently she co-organised the WebNLG Shared Task, a challenge on generating text from RDF data.

Shashi Narayan is a research associate at the School of Informatics at the University of Edinburgh. His research focuses on natural language generation, understanding and structured predictions. A major aim of his research is to build on the hypothesis that tailoring a model with knowledge of the task structure and linguistic requirements, such as syntax and semantics, leads to a better performance. The questions raised in his research are relevant to various natural language applications such as question answering, paraphrase generation, semantic and syntactic parsing, document understanding and summarization, and text simplification. He mostly rely on machine learning techniques such as deep learning and spectral methods to develop NLP frameworks. His research has appeared in computational linguistics journals (e.g., TACL, Computational Linguistics and Pattern Recognition Letters) and in conferences (e.g., ACL, EMNLP, NAACL, COLING, EACL and INLG). He was nominated on the SIGGEN board (2012-14) as a student member. He co-organised the WebNLG Shared Task, a challenge on generating text from RDF data. Recently, he was nominated as an area co-chair for Generation at NAACL HLT 2018.

## 4 Audience, Previous Tutorials and Venue

Based on the recent upsurge of interest in NL generation as witnessed by the increase in submissions in that domain at the major NLP conferences, we target an audience of 60 to 100 students and researchers from both academia and industry. We are not aware of any recent tutorial on the topic of text production. Our preference for the venue is NAACL and EMNLP.

## References


[Bahdanau et al., 2014] Bahdanau, D., Cho, K., and Bengio, Y. (2014). Neural machine translation by jointly learning to align and translate. *CoRR*, abs/1409.0473.

[Bannard and Callison-Burch, 2005] Bannard, C. and Callison-Burch, C. (2005). Paraphrasing with bilingual parallel corpora. In *Proceedings of ACL*.

[Barzilay and McKeown, 2001] Barzilay, R. and McKeown, K. R. (2001). Extracting paraphrases from a parallel corpus. In *Proceedings of ACL*.

[Belz et al., 2011] Belz, A., White, M., Espinosa, D., Kow, E., Hogan, D., and Stent, A. (2011). The first surface realisation shared task: Overview and evaluation results. In *Proceedings of ENLG*.

[Celikyilmaz et al., 2018] Celikyilmaz, A., Bosselut, A., He, X., and Choi, Y. (2018). Deep communicating agents for abstractive summarization. In *Proceedings of the 16th Annual Conference of the North American Chapter of the Association for Computational Linguistics: Human Language Technologies*, New Orleans, US.

[Chen et al., 2016] Chen, Q., Zhu, X., Ling, Z., Wei, S., and Jiang, H. (2016). Distraction-based neural networks for modeling documents. In *Proceedings of IJCAI*, pages 2754–2760, New York, USA.

[Cheng and Lapata, 2016] Cheng, J. and Lapata, M. (2016). Neural summarization by extracting sentences and words. In *Proceedings of ACL*, pages 484–494, Berlin, Germany.

[Cohn and Lapata, 2008] Cohn, T. and Lapata, M. (2008). Sentence compression beyond word deletion. In *Proceedings of COLING*.

[Dong et al., 2017] Dong, L., Mallinson, J., Reddy, S., and Lapata, M. (2017). Learning to paraphrase for question answering. In *Proceedings of the 2017 Conference on Empirical Methods in Natural Language Processing*, pages 875–886, Copenhagen, Denmark.

[Dras, 1999] Dras, M. (1999). *Tree adjoining grammar and the reluctant paraphrasing of text*. PhD thesis, Macquarie University, Australia.

[Filippova, 2010] Filippova, K. (2010). Multi-sentence compression: Finding shortest paths in word graphs. In *Proceedings of COLING*.

[Filippova et al., 2015] Filippova, K., Alfonseca, E., Colmenares, C., Kaiser, L., and Vinyals, O. (2015). Sentence compression by deletion with LSTMs. In *Proceedings of EMNLP*.

[Filippova and Strube, 2008] Filippova, K. and Strube, M. (2008). Dependency tree based sentence compression. In *Proceedings of INLG*.

[Gardent et al., 2017a] Gardent, C., Shimorina, A., Narayan, S., and Perez-Beltrachini, L. (2017a). Creating training corpora for nlg micro-planning. In *Proceedings of ACL*.

[Gardent et al., 2017b] Gardent, C., Shimorina, A., Narayan, S., and Perez-Beltrachini, L. (2017b). The webnlg challenge: Generating text from rdf data. In *Proceedings of the 10th International Conference on Natural Language Generation*, pages 124–133.

[Knight and Marcu, 2000] Knight, K. and Marcu, D. (2000). Statistics-based summarization-step one: Sentence compression. In *Proceedings of AAAI-IAAI.*

[Konstas et al., 2017] Konstas, I., Iyer, S., Yatskar, M., Choi, Y., and Zettlemoyer, L. (2017). Neural amr: Sequence-to-sequence models for parsing and generation. In *Proceedings of ACL*, pages 146–157, Vancouver, Canada.

[Li et al., 2017] Li, J., Monroe, W., Shi, T., Jean, S., Ritter, A., and Jurafsky, D. (2017). Adversarial learning for neural dialogue generation. In *Proceedings of EMNLP*, pages 2157–2169.

[Mallinson et al., 2017] Mallinson, J., Sennrich, R., and Lapata, M. (2017). Paraphrasing revisited with neural machine translation. In *Proceedings of EACL.*

[May and Priyadarshi, 2017] May, J. and Priyadarshi, J. (2017). Semeval-2017 task 9: Abstract meaning representation parsing and generation. In *Proceedings of the 11th International Workshop on Semantic Evaluation (SemEval-2017)*, pages 536–545, Vancouver, Canada.

[McKeown et al., 2010] McKeown, K., Rosenthal, S., Thadani, K., and Moore, C. (2010). Time-efficient creation of an accurate sentence fusion corpus. In *Proceedings of NAACL-HLT.*

[Mille et al., 2018] Mille, S., Bohnet, B., Wanner, L., Belz, A., and Pitler, E. (2018). Surface realization shared task 2018: The generation challenges. In *To appear in Multilingual Surface Realization Workshop at ACL 2018.*

[Nallapati et al., 2017] Nallapati, R., Zhai, F., and Zhou, B. (2017). Summarunner: A recurrent neural network based sequence model for extractive summarization of documents. In *Proceedings of AAAI*, pages 3075–3081, San Francisco, California USA.

[Nallapati et al., 2016] Nallapati, R., Zhou, B., dos Santos, C. N., Gülçehre, Ç., and Xiang, B. (2016). Abstractive text summarization using sequence-to-sequence RNNs and beyond. In *Proceedings of CoNLL*, pages 280–290, Berlin, Germany.

[Narayan et al., 2018a] Narayan, S., Cardenas, R., Papasarantopoulos, N., Cohen, S. B., Lapata, M., Yu, J., and Chang, Y. (2018a). Document modeling with external attention for sentence extraction. In *Proceedings of the 56st Annual Meeting of the Association for Computational Linguistics*, Melbourne, Australia.

[Narayan et al., 2018b] Narayan, S., Cohen, S. B., and Lapata, M. (2018b). Ranking sentences for extractive summarization with reinforcement learning. In *Proceedings of the 16th Annual Conference of the North American Chapter of the Association for Computational Linguistics: Human Language Technologies*, New Orleans, US.

[Narayan and Gardent, 2014] Narayan, S. and Gardent, C. (2014). Hybrid simplification using deep semantics and machine translation. In *Proceedings of ACL.*

[Narayan and Gardent, 2016] Narayan, S. and Gardent, C. (2016). Unsupervised sentence simplification using deep semantics. In *Proceedings of INLG.*

[Narayan et al., 2017] Narayan, S., Gardent, C., Cohen, S. B., and Shimorina, A. (2017). Split and rephrase. In *Proceedings of EMNLP*, pages 606–616, Copenhagen, Denmark.

[Narayan et al., 2016] Narayan, S., Reddy, S., and Cohen, S. B. (2016). Paraphrase generation from latent-variable pcfgs for semantic parsing. In *Proceedings of the 9th International Natural Language Generation conference*, pages 153–162, Edinburgh, UK.

[Nenkova and McKeown, 2011] Nenkova, A. and McKeown, K. (2011). Automatic summarization. *Foundations and Trends in Information Retrieval*, 5(2–3):103–233.

[Novikova et al., 2017] Novikova, J., Dušek, O., and Rieser, V. (2017). The E2E dataset: New challenges for end-to-end generation. In *Proceedings of the 18th Annual Meeting of the Special Interest Group on Discourse and Dialogue*, Saarbrücken, Germany. arXiv:1706.09254.

[Pasunuru and Bansal, 2018] Pasunuru, R. and Bansal, M. (2018). Multi-reward reinforced summarization with saliency and entailment. In *Proceedings of the 16th Annual Conference of the North American Chapter of the Association for Computational Linguistics: Human Language Technologies*, New Orleans, US.

[Paulus et al., 2017] Paulus, R., Xiong, C., and Socher, R. (2017). A deep reinforced model for abstractive summarization. *CoRR*, abs/1705.04304.

[Pitler, 2010] Pitler, E. (2010). Methods for sentence compression. Technical report, University of Pennsylvania.

[Rush et al., 2015] Rush, A. M., Chopra, S., and Weston, J. (2015). A neural attention model for abstractive sentence summarization. In *Proceedings of EMNLP*, pages 379–389, Lisbon, Portugal.

[See et al., 2017] See, A., Liu, P. J., and Manning, C. D. (2017). Get to the point: Summarization with pointer-generator networks. In *Proceedings of ACL*, pages 1073–1083, Vancouver, Canada.

[Shang et al., 2015] Shang, L., Lu, Z., and Li, H. (2015). Neural responding machine for short-text conversation. *CoRR*, abs/1503.02364.

[Siddharthan et al., 2004] Siddharthan, A., Nenkova, A., and McKeown, K. (2004). Syntactic simplification for improving content selection in multi-document summarization. In *Proceedings of COLING*.

[Song et al., ] Song, L., Zhang, Y., Wang, Z., and Gildea, D.

[Sutskever et al., 2011] Sutskever, I., Martens, J., and Hinton, G. E. (2011). Generating text with recurrent neural networks. In *Proceedings of ICML*.

[Tan and Wan, 2017] Tan, J. and Wan, X. (2017). Abstractive document summarization with a graph-based attentional neural model. In *Proceedings of ACL*, pages 1171–1181, Vancouver, Canada.

[Thadani and McKeown, 2013] Thadani, K. and McKeown, K. (2013). Supervised sentence fusion with single-stage inference. In *Proceedings of IJCNLP*.

[Toutanova et al., 2016] Toutanova, K., Brockett, C., Tran, K. M., and Amershi, S. (2016). A dataset and evaluation metrics for abstractive compression of sentences and short paragraphs. In *Proceedings of EMNLP*.

[Vinyals et al., 2015] Vinyals, O., Fortunato, M., and Jaitly, N. (2015). Pointer networks. In *Advances in Neural Information Processing Systems 28*, pages 2692–2700.

[Wan, 2010] Wan, X. (2010). Towards a unified approach to simultaneous single-document and multi-document summarizations. In *Proceedings of COLING*, pages 1137–1145, Beijing, China.

[Wen et al., 2016] Wen, T.-H., Gašić, M., Mrkšić, N., Rojas-Barahona, L. M., Su, P.-H., Vandyke, D., and Young, S. (2016). Multi-domain neural network language generation for spoken dialogue systems. In *Proceedings of NAACL-HLT*.

[Wen et al., 2015] Wen, T.-H., Gašić, M., Mrkšić, N., Su, P.-H., Vandyke, D., and Young, S. (2015). Semantically conditioned LSTM-based natural language generation for spoken dialogue systems. In *Proceedings of EMNLP*.

[Woodsend and Lapata, 2010] Woodsend, K. and Lapata, M. (2010). Automatic generation of story highlights. In *Proceedings of ACL*, pages 565–574, Uppsala, Sweden.

[Woodsend and Lapata, 2011] Woodsend, K. and Lapata, M. (2011). Learning to simplify sentences with quasi-synchronous grammar and integer programming. In *Proceedings of EMNLP*.

[Wubben et al., 2010] Wubben, S., Van Den Bosch, A., and Krahmer, E. (2010). Paraphrase generation as monolingual translation: Data and evaluation. In *Proceedings of INLG*.

[Wubben et al., 2012] Wubben, S., van den Bosch, A., and Krahmer, E. (2012). Sentence simplification by monolingual machine translation. In *Proceedings of ACL*.

[Xu et al., 2015] Xu, W., Callison-Burch, C., and Napoles, C. (2015). Problems in current text simplification research: New data can help. *Transactions of the Association for Computational Linguistics*, 3:283–297.

[Yasunaga et al., 2017] Yasunaga, M., Zhang, R., Meelu, K., Pareek, A., Srinivasan, K., and Radev, D. (2017). Graph-based neural multi-document summarization. In *Proceedings of CoNLL*, pages 452–462, Vancouver, Canada.

[Zhang and Lapata, 2017] Zhang, X. and Lapata, M. (2017). Sentence simplification with deep reinforcement learning. In *Proceedings of EMNLP*.

[Zhu et al., 2010] Zhu, Z., Bernhard, D., and Gurevych, I. (2010). A monolingual tree-based translation model for sentence simplification. In *Proceedings of COLING*.

# Scalable Construction and Reasoning of Massive Knowledge Bases

**— Proposal for a Tutorial at NAACL 2018 —**

**Xiang Ren**[1] **Nanyun Peng**[2] **William Yang Wang** [3]
[1] University of Southern California, Department of Computer Science
[2] University of Southern California, Information Sciences Institute
[3] University of California, Santa Barbara, Department of Computer Science
xiangren@usc.edu, npeng@isi.edu, william@cs.ucsb.edu

## Abstract

In today's information-based society, there is abundant knowledge out there carried in the form of natural language texts (e.g., news articles, social media posts, scientific publications), which spans across various domains (*e.g.*, corporate documents, advertisements, legal acts, medical reports), and grows at an astonishing rate. How to turn such massive and unstructured text data into structured, actionable knowledge for computational machines, and furthermore, how to teach machines learn to reason and complete the extracted knowledge is a grand challenge to the research community.

Traditional IE systems assume abundant human annotations for training high quality machine learning models, which is impractical when trying to deploy IE systems to a broad range of domains, settings and languages.

In the first part of the tutorial, we introduce how to extract structured facts (*i.e.*, entities and their relations of different types) from text corpora to construct knowledge bases, with a focus on methods that are minimally-supervised and domain-independent for timely knowledge base construction across various application domains.

In the second part, we introduce how to leverage other knowledge, such as the distributional statistics of characters and words, the annotations for other tasks and other domains, and the linguistics and problem structures, to combat the problem of inadequate supervision, and conduct low-resource information extraction.

In the third part, we describe recent advances in knowledge base reasoning. We start with the gentle introduction to the literature, focusing on path-based and embedding based methods. We then describe DeepPath, a recent attempt of using deep reinforcement learning to combine the best of both worlds for knowledge base reasoning.

## 1 Introduction

**Motivation.** The success of data mining and artificial intelligence technology is largely attributed to the efficient and effective analysis of structured data. The construction of a well-structured, machine-actionable knowledge base (KB) from raw (unstructured or loosely-structured) data sources is often the premise of consequent applications. Although the majority of existing data generated in our society is unstructured, big data leads to big opportunities to uncover structures of real-world entities (*e.g.*, `person`, `product`), attributes (*e.g.*, `age`, `weight`), relations (*e.g.*, `employee_of`, `manufacture`) from massive text corpora. By integrating these semantic structures, one can construct a powerful KB as a conceptual abstraction of the original corpus. The constructed knowledge base will facilitate browsing information and inferring knowledge that are otherwise widely scattered in the text corpora. Computational machines can effectively perform algorithmic analysis at a large scale over these KBs, and apply the new insights to improve human productivity in various downstream tasks.



*Proceedings of NAACL-HLT 2018: Tutorial Abstracts*, pages 10–16
New Orleans, Louisiana, June 1, 2018. 

**Our Focus.** In this tutorial, we focus our discussion on two tightly related problems: automatic construction of knowledge bases from text, and knowledge reasoning for knowledge base completion. While traditional information extraction techniques have heavy reliance on human-annotated data, our tutorial will devote more time on introducing methods that can reduce human efforts in the process, by leveraging external knowledge sources (e.g., distant supervision) and exploiting rich data redundancy in massive text corpora (e.g., weak supervision). We also discuss how data sources from various domains and languages could opens up tremendous opportunities to leverage and transfer existing knowledge about domains, tasks and language, and help knowledge extraction in low-resource settings with minimal supervision. In the reasoning part, we aim to leverage the existing background knowledge and design various algorithms to fill in the missing link between entities in the KB, given the extracted KBs are likely incomplete. More specifically, this part will introduce two lines of research for KB reasoning: path-based and embedding-based methods.

**Topics to be covered in this tutorial.** The first 2/3 of this tutorial presents a comprehensive overview of the information extraction techniques developed in recent years for constructing knowledge bases (see also Section 2 for a more detailed outline). We will discuss the following key issues: (1) data-driven approaches for mining quality phrases from massive, unstructured text corpora; (2) entity recognition and typing: preliminaries, challenges, and methodologies; and (3) relation extraction: previous efforts, limitations, recent progress, and a joint entity and relation extraction method using distant supervision; (4) multi-task and multi-domain learning for low-resource information extraction; (5) distill linguistic knowledge into neural models to help low-resource information extraction. The second half of the tutorial presents a comprehensive overview of KB reasoning techniques. For path-based methods, we will first describe the Path-Ranking Algorithm (PRA) (Lao et al., 2011) and briefly describe extensions such as ProPPR (Wang et al., 2013). Our tutorial will also cover the recent integration of PRA with recurrent neural networks. For the embedding based method, we will briefly describe RESCAL (Nickel et al., 2011) and TransE (Bordes et al., 2013). Finally, we discuss DeepPath (Xiong et al., 2017), a novel deep reinforcement learning model that combines the embedding and path-based approaches for the learning to reason problem.

**Research Impact.** Our phrase mining tool, SegPhrase (Liu et al., 2015), won the grand prize of Yelp Dataset Challenge[1] and was used by TripAdvisor in productions[2]. Our entity recognition and typing system, ClusType (Ren et al., 2015), was shipped as part of the products in Microsoft Bing and U.S. Army Research Lab. We built the first named entity recognizer on Chinese social media (Peng and Dredze, 2015, 2016) and closed the gap between NER on English and Chinese social media. The same technique was applied to build the first relation extractor for cross-sentence, n-ary relation extraction between drug, gene, and mutation (Peng et al., 2017).

**Duration and Sessions.** The duration of the tutorial is flexible: It is expected to be 3 hours, but it can be extended into 6 hours, based on the need of the conference. The outline presented here is for the 3-hour tutorial. For longer duration of the tutorial, we plan to extend entity and relation extraction parts, and add in more case studies and applications.

**Relevance to ACL.** Machine "reading" and "reasoning" of large text corpora have long been the interests to CL and NLP communities, especially when people now are exposed to an explosion of information in the form of free text. Extracting structured information is key to understanding messy and scattered raw data, and effective reasoning tools are critical for the use of KBs in downstream tasks like QA. This tutorial will present an organized picture of recent research on knowledge base construction and reasoning. We will show how exciting and surprising knowledge can be discovered from your own not so well-structured raw corpora, and such incomplete KBs can be further used to derive new insights and more complex knowledge with reasoning techniques.

[1] http://www.yelp.com/dataset_challenge

[2] http://engineering.tripadvisor.com/mining-text-review-snippets/

## 2 Outline

This tutorial presents a comprehensive overview of techniques for automatic knowledge base construction from text data (especially from a large, domain-specific text corpora), and techniques for reasoning over large-scale knowledge bases. We will discuss the following key issues:

1. Overview
   (a) Knowledge base: A little history
   (b) Knowledge base preliminaries
   (c) Knowledge base construction: An overview
      i. From phrases to entities and relations
2. Phrase Mining from Massive Text Corpora
   (a) Preliminaries
      i. Criteria of Quality Phrases
      ii. The Origin of Phrase Mining
         A. Automatic Term Recognition
         B. Supervised Noun Phrase Chunking
         C. Dependency Parser-based Methods
   (b) Data-Driven Phrase Mining in A Large Text Corpus
      i. Unsupervised Frequency-based Methods
      ii. Weakly Supervised Method: SegPhrase
      iii. Automated Quality Phrase
         A. No Extra Human Effort
         B. Support Multiple Languages
         C. High Performance
3. Automated Entity Recognition and Typing
   (a) Preliminaries
      i. Entities that are explicitly typed and linked externally with documents.
         A. Wikilinks and ClueWeb corpora
         B. Probase: A Probabilistic Taxonomy
         C. MENED: Mining evidence outside referent knowledge bases
      ii. Entities that can be extracted within text.
      iii. Traditional named entity recognition (NER) systems
         A. Entity extraction as a sequence labeling task
         B. Classic coarse types and manually-annotated corpora
         C. Sequence labeling models
   (b) Entity Recognition and Typing in A Large, Domain-specific Corpus
      i. Semi-supervised approaches
         A. Combining local and global features
      ii. Weakly-supervised approaches
         A. Pattern-based bootstrapping methods
         B. SEISA: A set expansion method
         C. Extracting entities from web tables
      iii. Distantly-supervised approaches
         A. SemTagger: Seed-based contextual classifier for entity typing
         B. ClusType: Effective entity recognition by relation phrase-based clustering
      iv. Fine-grained entity typing approaches
         A. FIGER: Multi-label classification with automatically annotated data
         B. Embedding methods for entity typing: AFET and WSABIE
      v. Label noise reduction in distant supervision
         A. Noisy type issue in distant supervision
         B. Simple pruning heuristics
         C. Partial-label learning methods
         D. Label noise reduction by heterogeneous partial-label embedding
4. Automated Extraction of Structured Entity Relationships
   (a) Preliminaries of relation extraction (RE)
      i. Basic concepts: relation instance, relation mention
      ii. Explicit relation vs. implicit relation
      iii. Downstream applications
         A. Knowledge base completion
         B. Question answering systems
   (b) Traditional supervised RE systems
      i. Supervised RE methods
         A. Supervised models
         B. Features for relation extraction
         C. Training data
         D. Evaluation of RE task
      ii. Systems from Stanford and IBM
   (c) Extracting typed relations from A Massive Corpus
      i. Weak supervision methods

A. Pattern-based boostrapping methods
B. Seed examples selection
C. DIPRE system
D. KnowItAll system
E. Snowball system

ii. Distant supervision (DS) methods
A. Distant supervision for RE: A typical workflow
B. Challenges of DS: noisy candidate labels
C. Noise-robust DS models

iii. Joint extraction of entities and relations
A. Supervised methods: linear programming and sequence models
B. CoType: A distantly-supervised method

5. Transfer Knowledge for Low Resource Information Extraction

(a) Multi-task and multi-domain learning for named entity recognition
(b) Cross-lingual entity extraction
(c) Distilling linguistics knowledge into relation extraction system

6. Knowledge Base Reasoning: Background and State-of-the-Arts

(a) Preliminaries
i. KB Reasoning and Information Extraction
A. Difference with IE
ii. Challenges of KB Reasoning
A. Noisy Background Knowledge
B. Combinatorial explosion and huge search space
C. Scalability

(b) Path-Based Approaches
i. The Path-Finding Algorithm
ii. ProPPR
iii. Combining PRA and Recurrent Neural Networks

(c) Embedding-Based Approaches
i. RESCAL
ii. TransE
iii. Other Recent Studies

(d) DeepPath: Reinforcement Learning for KB Reasoning
i. Problem Formulation
ii. The DeepPath Algorithm
iii. Imitation Learning
iv. Experimental Results

7. Research Frontier

## 3 Organizers

**Xiang Ren**, Assistant Professor, Department of Computer Science, University of Southern California. His research focuses on creating computational tools for better understanding and exploring massive text data. He has published over 25 papers in major conferences. He received Google PhD Fellowship, KDD Rising Star by Microsoft, Yahoo!-DAIS Research Excellence Award, C. W. Gear Outstanding Graduate Student Award by UIUC and Yelp Dataset Challenge Award. Mr. Ren has rich experiences in delivering tutorials in major conferences, including SIGKDD 2015, SIGMOD 2016 and WWW 2017. Homepage: `http://xren7.web.engr.illinois.edu/`.

**Nanyun Peng** is a Research Assistant Professor at the Department of Computer Science, and a Computer Scientist at the Information Sciences Institute, University of Southern California. She is broadly interested in Natural Language Processing, Machine Learning, and Information Extraction. Her research focuses on low-resource information extraction, creative language generation, and phonology/morphology modeling. Nanyun is the recipient of the Johns Hopkins University 2016 Fred Jelinek Fellowship. She has a background in computational linguistics and economics and holds BAs in both. Home page: `http://www.vnpeng.net`.

**William Wang** is an Assistant Professor at the Department of Computer Science, University of California, Santa Barbara. He received his PhD from Carnegie Mellon University, where he worked on scalable probabilistic reasoning language ProPPR with William Cohen. He focuses on information extraction and he is the faculty author of DeepPath—the first deep reinforcement learning system for multi-hop knowledge reasoning. He has published more than 40 papers at leading conferences and journals including *ACL, EMNLP, NAACL, COLING, IJCAI, CIKM, SIGDIAL, IJCNLP, INTERSPEECH,*

*ICASSP, ASRU, SLT, Machine Learning, and Computer Speech & Language*, and he has received paper awards and honors from CIKM, ASRU, and EMNLP. Website: `http://www.cs.ucsb.edu/~william/`.

## 4 Previous Editions and Related Tutorials

A list of tutorials on the most related topics:

1. **Conference tutorial:** X. Ren, Y. Su, X. Yan, "Construction and Querying of Large-scale Knowledge Bases" (CIKM'17). `http://xren7.web.engr.illinois.edu/tutorial-cikm17.html`.
2. **Conference tutorial:** J. Pujara, S. Singh, B. Dalvi, "Knowledge Graph Construction From Text" (AAAI'17). `https://kgtutorial.github.io/`.
3. **Conference tutorial:** X. Ren, M. Jiang, J. Shang and J. Han, "Constructing Structured Information Networks from Massive Text Corpora" (WWW'17). `http://xren7.web.engr.illinois.edu/www17tutorial.html`.
4. **Conference tutorial:** W. Y. Wang, W. Cohen "Scalable Probabilistic Logics" (IJCAI'16). `http://www.cs.cmu.edu/~yww/tutorials.html`.
5. **Conference tutorial:** W. Y. Wang, W. Cohen "Statistical Relational Learning for NLP" (NAACL'16). `http://www.aclweb.org/anthology/N16-4005`.
6. **Conference tutorial:** E. Gabrilovichn, N. Usunier, "Constructing and Mining Web-scale Knowledge Graphs" (SIGIR'16). `http://dl.acm.org/citation.cfm?id=2914807/`.
7. **Conference tutorial:** X. Ren, A. El-Kishky, C. Wang and J. Han, "Automatic Entity Recognition and Typing in Massive Text Corpora" (WWW'16). `http://web.engr.illinois.edu/~elkishk2/www2016/`.
8. **Conference tutorial:** X. Ren, A. El-Kishky, C. Wang and J. Han, "Automatic Entity Recognition and Typing from Massive Text Corpora: A Phrase and Network Mining Approach" (SIGKDD'15). `http://research.microsoft.com/en-us/people/chiw/kdd15tutorial.aspx`.

Most of the previous tutorials focused exclusively on the knowledge base construction aspect. In the proposed tutorial, we will give a systematic discussion on the problem of knowledge base reasoning, for which extensive studies have been conducted recently but systematic tutorials are lacking. This tutorial also presents recent advances in applying distant and weak supervision to the extraction of structured facts in knowledge base construction, in addition to the traditional supervised techniques and rule-based approaches.

**Target audience and prerequisites.** Researchers and practitioners in the field of natural language processing, computational linguistic, text mining, information retrieval, semantic web and machine learning. While the audience with a good background in these areas would benefit most from this tutorial, we believe the material to be presented would give general audience and newcomers an introductory pointer to the current work and important research topics in this field, and inspire them to learn more. Only preliminary knowledge about NLP, algorithms and their applications are needed. We expect there will be around 70 people interested in our tutorial.

**Tutorial material and equipment.** We will provide attendees a website and upload our tutorial materials (slides, references, softwares). There is no copyright issue. Standard equipment will be enough for our tutorial.

## References


Eugene Agichtein and Luis Gravano. 2000. Snowball: Extracting relations from large plain-text collections. In *ACM conference on Digital libraries*. pages 85–94.

Nguyen Bach and Sameer Badaskar. 2007. A review of relation extraction. *Literature review for Language and Statistics II* .

Kurt Bollacker, Colin Evans, Praveen Paritosh, Tim Sturge, and Jamie Taylor. 2008. Freebase: a collaboratively created graph database for structuring human knowledge. In *SIGMOD*.

Antoine Bordes, Nicolas Usunier, Alberto Garcia-Duran, Jason Weston, and Oksana Yakhnenko. 2013. Translating embeddings for modeling multi-relational data. In *Advances in neural information processing systems*. pages 2787–2795.

Andrew Carlson, Justin Betteridge, Richard C Wang, Estevam R Hruschka Jr, and Tom M Mitchell. 2010. Coupled semi-supervised learning for information extraction. In *WSDM*.

Oren Etzioni, Michael Cafarella, Doug Downey, Stanley Kok, Ana-Maria Popescu, Tal Shaked, Stephen Soderland, Daniel S Weld, and Alexander Yates. 2004. Web-scale information extraction in knowitall:(preliminary results). In *Proceedings of the 13th international conference on World Wide Web*. ACM, pages 100–110.

Venkatesh Ganti, Arnd C König, and Rares Vernica. 2008. Entity categorization over large document collections. In *SIGKDD*.

Sonal Gupta and Christopher D. Manning. 2014. Improved pattern learning for bootstrapped entity extraction. In *CONLL*.

Yeye He and Dong Xin. 2011. Seisa: set expansion by iterative similarity aggregation. In *WWW*.

Raphael Hoffmann, Congle Zhang, Xiao Ling, Luke Zettlemoyer, and Daniel S Weld. 2011. Knowledge-based weak supervision for information extraction of overlapping relations. In *ACL*.

Ruihong Huang and Ellen Riloff. 2010. Inducing domain-specific semantic class taggers from (almost) nothing. In *ACL*.

Terry Koo, Xavier Carreras, and Michael Collins. 2008. Simple semi-supervised dependency parsing. *ACL-HLT* .

Ni Lao, Tom Mitchell, and William W Cohen. 2011. Random walk inference and learning in a large scale knowledge base. In *Proceedings of the Conference on Empirical Methods in Natural Language Processing*. Association for Computational Linguistics, pages 529–539.

Qi Li and Heng Ji. 2014. Incremental joint extraction of entity mentions and relations. In *ACL*.

Yang Li, Chi Wang, Fangqiu Han, Jiawei Han, Dan Roth, and Xifeng Yan. 2013. Mining evidences for named entity disambiguation. In *Proceedings of the 19th ACM SIGKDD international conference on Knowledge discovery and data mining*. ACM, pages 1070–1078.

Girija Limaye, Sunita Sarawagi, and Soumen Chakrabarti. 2010. Annotating and searching web tables using entities, types and relationships. *VLDB* 3(1-2):1338–1347.

Xiao Ling and Daniel S Weld. 2012. Fine-grained entity recognition. In *AAAI*.

Jialu Liu, Jingbo Shang, Chi Wang, Xiang Ren, and Jiawei Han. 2015. Mining quality phrases from massive text corpora. In *SIGMOD*.

Ryan McDonald, Fernando Pereira, Kiril Ribarov, and Jan Hajič. 2005. Non-projective dependency parsing using spanning tree algorithms. In *EMNLP*.

Paul McNamee and James Mayfield. 2002. Entity extraction without language-specific resources. In *proceedings of the 6th conference on Natural language learning-Volume 20*. Association for Computational Linguistics, pages 1–4.

Mike Mintz, Steven Bills, Rion Snow, and Dan Jurafsky. 2009. Distant supervision for relation extraction without labeled data. In *ACL*.

Maximilian Nickel, Volker Tresp, and Hans-Peter Kriegel. 2011. A three-way model for collective learning on multi-relational data. In *ICML*. volume 11, pages 809–816.

Nanyun Peng and Mark Dredze. 2015. Named entity recognition for chinese social media with jointly trained embeddings. In *Proceedings of the 2015 Conference on Empirical Methods in Natural Language Processing (EMNLP)*. Lisboa, Portugal.

Nanyun Peng and Mark Dredze. 2016. Improving named entity recognition for chinese social media via learning segmentation representations .

Nanyun Peng, Hoifung Poon, Chris Quirk, Kristina Toutanova, and Wen-tau Yih. 2017. Cross-sentence n-ary relation extraction with graph lstms. *Transactions of the Association for Computational Linguistics* 5:101–115.

Vasin Punyakanok and Dan Roth. 2001. The use of classifiers in sequential inference. In *NIPS*.

Lev Ratinov and Dan Roth. 2009. Design challenges and misconceptions in named entity recognition. In *ACL*.

Xiang Ren, Ahmed El-Kishky, Chi Wang, Fangbo Tao, Clare R. Voss, and Jiawei Han. 2015. ClusType: Effective entity recognition and typing by relation phrase-based clustering. In *KDD*.

Xiang Ren, Wenqi He, Meng Qu, Lifu Huang, Heng Ji, and Jiawei Han. 2016a. AFET: Automatic fine-grained entity typing by hierarchical partial-label embedding. In *EMNLP*.

Xiang Ren, Wenqi He, Meng Qu, Clare R Voss, Heng Ji, and Jiawei Han. 2016b. Label noise reduction in entity typing by heterogeneous partial-label embedding. In *KDD*.

Xiang Ren, Zeqiu Wu, Wenqi He, Meng Qu, Clare R. Voss, Heng Ji, Tarek F. Abdelzaher, and Jiawei Han. 2017. CoType: Joint extraction of typed entities and relations with knowledge bases. In *arXiv:1610.08763*.

Wei Shen, Jianyong Wang, and Jiawei Han. 2014. Entity linking with a knowledge base: Issues, techniques, and solutions. *TKDE* (99):1–20.

Yu Su, Huan Sun, Brian Sadler, Mudhakar Srivatsa, Izzeddin Gur, Zenghui Yan, and Xifeng Yan. 2016. On generating characteristic-rich question sets for qa evaluation. In *EMNLP*. pages 562–572.

Yizhou Sun and Jiawei Han. 2013. Mining heterogeneous information networks: a structural analysis approach. *SIGKDD Explorations* 14(2):20–28.

Jian Tang, Meng Qu, and Qiaozhu Mei. 2015. Pte: Predictive text embedding through large-scale heterogeneous text networks. In *Proceedings of the 21th ACM SIGKDD International Conference on Knowledge Discovery and Data Mining*. ACM, pages 1165–1174.

Joseph Turian, Lev Ratinov, and Yoshua Bengio. 2010. Word representations: a simple and general method for semi-supervised learning. In *ACL*.

William Yang Wang, Kathryn Mazaitis, and William W Cohen. 2013. Programming with personalized pagerank: a locally groundable first-order probabilistic logic. In *Proceedings of the 22nd ACM international conference on Information & Knowledge Management*. ACM, pages 2129–2138.

Wentao Wu, Hongsong Li, Haixun Wang, and Kenny Q Zhu. 2012. Probase: A probabilistic taxonomy for text understanding. In *Proceedings of the 2012 ACM SIGMOD International Conference on Management of Data*. ACM, pages 481–492.

Wenhan Xiong, Thien Hoang, and William Yang Wang. 2017. Deeppath: A reinforcement learning method for knowledge graph reasoning. *EMNLP* .

Endong Xun, Changning Huang, and Ming Zhou. 2000. A unified statistical model for the identification of english basenp. In *ACL*.

Mohamed Yakout, Kris Ganjam, Kaushik Chakrabarti, and Surajit Chaudhuri. 2012. Infogather: entity augmentation and attribute discovery by holistic matching with web tables. In *SIGMOD*.

GuoDong Zhou, Jian Su, Jie Zhang, and Min Zhang. 2005. Exploring various knowledge in relation extraction. In *ACL*.

# The interplay between lexical resources and Natural Language Processing


## Abstract

Incorporating linguistic, world and common sense knowledge into AI/NLP systems is currently an important research area, with several open problems and challenges. At the same time, processing and storing this knowledge in lexical resources is not a straightforward task. We propose to address these complementary goals from two methodological perspectives: the use of NLP methods to help the process of constructing and enriching lexical resources and the use of lexical resources for improving NLP applications. This tutorial may be useful for two main types of audience: those working on language resources who are interested in becoming acquainted with automatic NLP techniques, with the end goal of speeding and/or easing up the process of resource curation; and on the other hand, researchers in NLP who would like to benefit from the knowledge of lexical resources to improve their systems and models.


## 1. Description

The manual construction of lexical resources is a prohibitively time-consuming process, and even in the most restricted knowledge domains and less-resourced languages, the use of language technologies to ease up this process is becoming a standard practice. NLP techniques can be effectively leveraged to reduce creation and maintenance efforts. In this tutorial we will present open problems and research challenges in these topics concerning the interplay between lexical resources and NLP. Additionally, we will summarize existing attempts in this direction, such as modeling linguistic phenomena like terminology, definitions and glosses, examples and relations, phraseological units, or clustering techniques for senses and topics, as well as the integration of resources of different nature. The following topics are going to be covered in detail:

- **Terminology extraction.** Measures for terminology extraction, the simple conventional tf-idf (Sparck Jones, 1972), lexical specificity (Lafon, 1980), and more recent approaches exploiting linguistic knowledge (Hulth 2003; Vivaldi and Rodríguez, 2010).

- **Definition extraction.** Techniques for extracting definitional text snippets from corpora (Navigli and Velardi, 2010; Boella and DiCaro, 2013; Espinosa-Anke et al. 2015; Li et al. 2016).




*Proceedings of NAACL-HLT 2018: Tutorial Abstracts*, pages 17–23
New Orleans, Louisiana, June 1, 2018.

- **Automatic extraction of examples.** Description of example extraction techniques and designs on this direction, e.g., the GDEX criteria and their implementation (Kilgariff et al., 2008).

- **Information extraction.** Recent approaches for extracting semantic relations from text: NELL (Carlson et al., 2010), ReVerb (Fader et al. 2011), PATTY (Nakashole et al., 2011), KB-Unify (Delli Bovi et al., 2015).

- **Hypernym discovery and taxonomy learning.** Insights from recent SemEval tasks (Bordea et al. 2015, 2016) and related efforts on the automatic extraction of hypernymy relations from text corpora (Velardi et al. 2013; Alfarone and Davis 2015; Flati et al. 2016; Shwartz et al. 2016; Espinosa-Anke et al. 2016a; Gupta et al. 2016).

- **Topic clustering techniques**. Relevant techniques for filtering general domain resources via topic grouping (Roget's, 1911; Navigli and Velardi, 2004, Camacho-Collados and Navigli, 2017).

- **Alignment of lexical resources:** Alignment of heterogeneous lexical resources contributing to the creation of large resources containing different sources of knowledge. We will present approaches for the construction of such resources, such as Yago (Suchanek et al. 2007), UBY (Gurevych et al. 2012), BabelNet (Navigli and Ponzetto, 2012) or ConceptNet (Speer et al. 2017), as well as other works attempting to improve the automatic procedures to align lexical resources (Matuschek and Gurevych, 2013; Pilehvar and Navigli, 2014).

- **Ontology enrichment.** Enriching lexical ontologies with novel synsets or with additional relations (Jurgens and Pilehvar, 2015; 2016; Espinosa-Anke et al., 2016b).

In addition to these automatic efforts for easing the task of constructing and enriching lexical resources, we will present NLP tasks in which lexical resources have shown an important contribution. Effectively leveraging linguistically expressible cues with their associated knowledge remains a difficult task. Knowledge may be extracted from (roughly) three types of resources (Hovy et al., 2013): unstructured, e.g. text corpora; semistructured, such as encyclopedic collaborative repositories like Wikipedia and Wiktionary, or structured, which include lexicographic resources like WordNet or DBpedia.

We will explain some of the current challenges in Word Sense Disambiguation and Entity Linking, as key tasks in natural language understanding which also enable a direct integration of knowledge from lexical resources. We will explain some knowledge-based and supervised methods for these tasks which play a decisive role in connecting lexical resources and text data (Zhong and Ng, 2010; Agirre et al. 2014; Moro et al.. 2014; Ling et al. 2015; Raganato et al. 2017). Moreover, we will present the field of knowledge-based representations, in particular word sense embeddings (Chen et al. 2014; Rothe and Schuetze, 2015; Camacho-Collados et al. 2016; Pilehvar and Collier, 2016; Mancini et al. 2017), as flexible techniques which act as a bridge between lexical resources and applications. Finally, we will briefly present some recent work on the integration of this encoded knowledge from lexical resources into neural architectures for improving downstream NLP applications (Flekova and Gurevych, 2016; Pilehvar et al. 2017).

## 2. Outline

### ➢ Introduction and Motivation (15 mins)

Adding explicit knowledge into AI/NLP systems is currently an important challenge due to the gains that can be obtained in many downstream applications. At the same time, these resources can be further enriched and better exploited by making use of NLP techniques. In this context, the main motivation of this tutorial is to show how Natural Language Processing and Lexical Resources have interacted so far, and a view towards potential scenarios in the near future.

The tutorial is then divided in two main blocks. First, we delve into *NLP for Creation and Enrichment of Lexical Resources*, where we address a range of NLP problems aimed specifically at improving repositories of linguistically expressible knowledge. Second, we cover different use cases in which *Lexical Resources for NLP* have been leveraged successfully. The last part of the tutorial focuses on lessons learned from work in which we tried to reconcile both worlds, as well as our own view towards what the future holds for knowledge-based approaches to NLP.

### ➢ NLP for Lexical Resources (70 mins)

The application of language technologies to the automatic construction and extension of lexical resources has proven successful in that it has provided various tools for optimizing this often prohibitively costly and expensive process.. NLP techniques provide end-to-end technologies that can tackle all challenges in the language resource creation and maintenance pipeline.. In this tutorial we will summarize existing efforts in this direction, including the extraction from text of linguistic phenomena like terminology, definitions and glosses, examples and relations, as well as clustering techniques for senses and topics. We will additionally summarize recent work on the automatic integration of knowledge from heterogeneous resources such as BabelNet, ConceptNet, Uby or Yago.

### [Coffee break] (20 mins)

### ➢ Lexical Resources for NLP (60 mins)

In this section we will present some of the applications on which lexical resources play an important role. In particular, we will explain some of the problems and challenges in Word Sense Disambiguation and Entity Linking, as key tasks in natural language understanding. Moreover, we will present the field of knowledge-based representations, in particular sense vectors and embeddings, as flexible techniques connecting lexical resources and downstream applications. We will additionally present some recent works on the integration of knowledge-based embeddings into neural architectures for improving downstream NLP applications.

### ➢ Open problems and challenges (15 mins)

In this last section we will introduce some of the open problems and challenges for automatizing the resource creation and enrichment process as well as for the integration of knowledge from lexical resources into NLP applications.

## 3. Instructors

**Jose Camacho Collados**
(camachocolladosj@cardiff.ac.uk; http://www.josecamachocollados.com) is a Research Associate at Cardiff University. Previously he was a Google Doctoral Fellow and completed his PhD at Sapienza University of Rome. His research focuses on Natural Language Processing and, more specifically, on the area of lexical and distributional semantics. Jose has experience in utilizing lexical resources for NLP applications, while enriching and improving these resources by extracting and processing knowledge from textual data. On this area he has co-organized the SemEval 2018 shared task on Hypernym Discovery. Previously, he co-organized a workshop on "Sense, Concept and Entity Representations and their Applications" at EACL 2017 and a tutorial on the same topic at ACL 2016. His background education includes an Erasmus Mundus Master in Natural Language Processing and Human Language Technology and a 5-year BSc degree in Mathematics.

**Luis Espinosa Anke**
(espinosa-ankel@cardiff.ac.uk, www.luisespinosa.net) received his BA in English Philology in 2006 (Univ. of Alicante, Spain), and his PhD in Natural Language Processing in 2017 (Univ. Pompeu Fabra, Spain). He holds two MAs, one in English-Spanish Translation (Univ. of Alicante), and an Erasmus Mundus MA in Natural Language Processing (NLP) (Univ. of Wolverhampton and Univ. Autònoma de Barcelona). His research interests lie in the intersection between structured representations of knowledge and NLP, specifically computational lexicography and distributional semantics. He has co-organized the SemEval 2018 shared tasks on Hypernym Discovery and Multilingual Emoji Prediction. Previously, he co-organized the Spanish NLP conference (2014) and the Focused NER task (Open Knowledge Extraction challenge) at ESWC 2017.

**Mohammad Taher Pilehvar**
(mp792@cam.ac.uk, http://people.ds.cam.ac.uk/mp792/) is a research associate at the University of Cambridge. Taher's research lies in lexical semantics, mainly focusing on semantic representation and similarity. In the past, he has co-instructed three tutorials on these topics (EMNLP 2015, ACL 2016, and EACL 2017) and co-organised three SemEval tasks. He has also co-authored several conference (including two ACL best paper nominations, at 2013 and 2017) and journal papers, including different semantic representation techniques based on heterogeneous lexical resources.

# References

Agirre, E., de Lacalle, O.L. and Soroa, A., 2014. Random walks for knowledge-based word sense disambiguation. Computational Linguistics, 40(1), pp.57-84.

Boella, G. and Di Caro, L., 2013, August. Extracting Definitions and Hypernym Relations relying on Syntactic Dependencies and Support Vector Machines. In ACL (2) (pp. 532-537).

Camacho-Collados, J., Pilehvar, M. T., & Navigli, R., 2016. Nasari: Integrating explicit knowledge and corpus statistics for a multilingual representation of concepts and entities. Artificial Intelligence, 240, 36-64.

Camacho-Collados, J. and Navigli, R., 2017. BabelDomains: Large-Scale Domain Labeling of Lexical Resources. EACL 2017, p.223.

Carlson, A., Betteridge, J., Kisiel, B., Settles, B., Hruschka Jr, E.R. and Mitchell, T.M., 2010, July. Toward an Architecture for Never-Ending Language Learning. In AAAI (Vol. 5, p. 3).

Chen, X., Liu, Z., & Sun, M., 2014. A Unified Model for Word Sense Representation and Disambiguation. In Proceedings of EMNLP (pp. 1025-1035).

Delli Bovi, C., Espinosa-Anke, L. and Navigli, R., 2015. Knowledge base unification via sense embeddings and disambiguation. In The 2015 Conference on Empirical Methods in Natural Language; Lisbon, Portugal. pp. 726-36.

Espinosa-Anke, L., Saggion, H. and Ronzano, F., 2015. Weakly supervised definition extraction. In Proceedings of the International Conference Recent Advances in Natural Language Processing (pp. 176-185).

Espinosa-Anke, L., Camacho-Collados, J., Bovi, C. D., & Saggion, H. (2016). Supervised distributional hypernym discovery via domain adaptation. In Proceedings of the 2016 Conference on Empirical Methods in Natural Language Processing (pp. 424-435).

Espinosa-Anke, L., Camacho-Collados, J., Rodríguez-Fernández, S., Saggion, H., & Wanner, L. (2016). Extending WordNet with Fine-Grained Collocational Information via Supervised

Distributional Learning. In Proceedings of COLING 2016, the 26th International Conference on Computational Linguistics: Technical Papers (pp. 3422-3432).

Fader, A., Soderland, S. and Etzioni, O., 2011. Identifying relations for open information extraction. In Proceedings of the Conference on Empirical Methods in Natural Language Processing (pp. 1535-1545). Association for Computational Linguistics.

Gurevych, I., Eckle-Kohler, J., Hartmann, S., Matuschek, M., Meyer, C. M., & Wirth, C., 2012. Uby: A large-scale unified lexical-semantic resource based on LMF. In Proceedings of EACL (pp. 580-590).

Kilgarriff, A., Husák, M., McAdam, K., Rundell, M. and Rychlý, P., 2008, July. GDEX: Automatically finding good dictionary examples in a corpus. In Proc. Euralex.

Flekova, L., & Gurevych, I., 2016. Supersense Embeddings: A Unified Model for Supersense Interpretation, Prediction, and Utilization. In Proceedings of ACL.

Hovy, E., Navigli, R. and Ponzetto, S.P., 2013. Collaboratively built semi-structured content and Artificial Intelligence: The story so far. Artificial Intelligence, 194, pp.2-27.

Hulth, A., 2003. Improved automatic keyword extraction given more linguistic knowledge. In Proceedings of the 2003 conference on Empirical methods in natural language processing (pp. 216-223). Association for Computational Linguistics.

Jurgens, D., & Pilehvar, M. T. (2015). Reserating the awesometastic: An automatic extension of the WordNet taxonomy for novel terms. In Proceedings of the 2015 Conference of the North American Chapter of the Association for Computational Linguistics: Human Language Technologies (pp. 1459-1465).

Jurgens, D., & Pilehvar, M. T. (2016). Semeval-2016 task 14: Semantic taxonomy enrichment. In Proceedings of the 10th International Workshop on Semantic Evaluation (SemEval-2016) (pp. 1092-1102).

Lafon, P., 1980. Sur la variabilité de la fréquence des formes dans un corpus. Mots, 1(1), pp.127-165.

Mancini, M., Camacho-Collados, J., Iacobacci, I., & Navigli, R., 2016. Embedding Words and Senses Together via Joint Knowledge-Enhanced Training. In Proceedings of CoNLL 2017.

Matuschek, M. & Gurevych, I., 2013. Dijkstra-wsa: A graph-based approach to word sense alignment. In Transactions of the Association for Computational Linguistics, 1, pp.151-164

Navigli, R. and Velardi, P., 2010. Learning word-class lattices for definition and hypernym extraction. In Proceedings of the 48th Annual Meeting of the Association for Computational Linguistics (pp. 1318-1327). Association for Computational Linguistics.

Navigli, R., & Ponzetto, S. P., 2012. BabelNet: The automatic construction, evaluation and application of a wide-coverage multilingual semantic network. Artificial Intelligence, 193, 217-250.

Pilehvar, M. T., & Collier, N., 2016. De-conflated semantic representations. In Proceedings of EMNLP.

Pilehvar, M. T., Camacho-Collados, J., Navigli, R., & Collier, N., 2017. Towards a Seamless Integration of Word Senses into Downstream NLP Applications. Proceedings of ACL.

Pilehvar, M.T. & Navigli, R., 2014. A robust approach to aligning heterogeneous lexical resources. In Proceedings of ACL.

Rothe, S., & Schütze, H., 2015. Autoextend: Extending word embeddings to embeddings for synsets and lexemes. In Proceedings of ACL.

Spark-Jones, K., 1972. A statistical interpretation of term specificity and its application in retrieval. Journal of documentation, 28(5), pp.111-121.

Speer, R., Chin, J. and Havasi, C., 2017. ConceptNet 5.5: An Open Multilingual Graph of General Knowledge. In AAAI (pp. 4444-4451).

Suchanek, F. M., Kasneci, G., & Weikum, G., 2007. Yago: a core of semantic knowledge. In Proceedings of the 16th international conference on World Wide Web (pp. 697-706). ACM.

Vivaldi, J. and Rodríguez, H., 2010. Finding Domain Terms using Wikipedia. In LREC.

Zhong, Z. and Ng, H.T., 2010. It makes sense: A wide-coverage word sense disambiguation system for free text. In Proceedings of the ACL 2010 System Demonstrations (pp. 78-83).

# Socially Responsible NLP

As language technologies have become increasingly prevalent, there is a growing awareness that decisions we make about our data, methods, and tools are often tied up with their impact on people and societies. This tutorial will provide an overview of real-world applications of language technologies and the potential ethical implications associated with them. We will discuss philosophical foundations of ethical research along with state-of-the art techniques. Discussion topics include:

- **Philosophical foundations:** what is ethics, history, medical and psychological experiments, IRB and human subjects, ethical decision making.
- **Misrepresentation and bias:** algorithms to identify biases in models and data and adversarial approaches to debiasing.
- **Civility in communication:** monitoring explicit abusive language and implicit microaggression.

Through this tutorial, we intend to provide the NLP researcher with an overview of tools to ensure that the data, algorithms, and models that they build are socially responsible. These tools will include a checklist of common pitfalls that one should avoid (e.g., demographic bias in data collection), as well as methods to adequately mitigate these issues (e.g., adjusting sampling rates or debiasing through regularization).

The tutorial is based on a new course on Ethics and NLP (http://demo.clab.cs.cmu.edu/ethical_nlp/) developed at Carnegie Mellon University.

You can learn more about the tutorial content and outline at https://sites.google.com/view/srnlp.

Additional relevant courses in the intersection of Ethics and NLP:

- Emily Bender at Univ. of Washington: http://faculty.washington.edu/ebender/2017_575/
- Graham Hirst at Univ. of Toronto: http://www.cs.utoronto.ca/~gh/cscD03/index.shtml

Readings relevant to tutorial preparation:

- https://goo.gl/7hA9D



*Proceedings of NAACL-HLT 2018: Tutorial Abstracts*, pages 24–26
New Orleans, Louisiana, June 1, 2018. 

## Outline

**Foundations**

- Motivation
- Philosophical foundations
- History: medical, psychological experiments, IRB and human subjects

**Bias and Misrepresentation in NLP**

- Psychological foundations of implicit bias
- Quantifying stereotypes, prejudice, and discrimination
- Debiasing

**Modeling Civility in Communication**

- Hate speech
- Implicit negativity: condescension
- Respect and formality in police-community communications

## Instructors

Yulia Tsvetkov, Carnegie Mellon University
ytsvetko@cs.cmu.edu
http://www.cs.cmu.edu/~ytsvetko/

Yulia Tsvetkov is an assistant professor in the Language Technologies Institute at Carnegie Mellon University. Her research interests lie at or near the intersection of natural language processing, machine learning, linguistics, and social science. Her current research projects focus on NLP for social good, including advancing language technologies for resource-poor languages spoken by millions of people, developing approaches to promote civility in communication (e.g., modeling gender bias in texts and debiasing), identifying strategies that undermine the democratic process (e.g., political framing and agenda-setting in digital media). Prior to joining CMU, Yulia was a postdoc in the Stanford NLP Group; she received her PhD from Carnegie Mellon University.

Vinodkumar Prabhakaran, Stanford University
vinod@cs.stanford.edu
www.cs.stanford.edu/~vinod

Vinodkumar Prabhakaran is currently a postdoctoral fellow at the Stanford NLP lab, and prior to this, received his PhD in Computer Science from Columbia University in 2015. In the fall, he will be starting as a research scientist at Google to work on issues around Ethics in AI and ML Fairness. His research falls in the interdisciplinary field of computational social sciences, with a focus on applying NLP for social good. He combines NLP techniques with social science methods in order to identify and address large scale societal issues, such as racial bias and disparities in law enforcement, manifestations of power and gender at workplace, and online incivility such as condescension and gender bias.

Rob Voigt, Stanford University
robvoigt@stanford.edu
https://nlp.stanford.edu/robvoigt/

Rob Voigt is a PhD student in the Linguistics Department at Stanford University, working on topics in computational sociolinguistics with Dan Jurafsky. His research focuses on using computational methods to understand how social context and social factors subtly influence linguistic behavior at a large scale. His dissertation is focused on techniques for extracting and analyzing linguistic implicit bias, including respectfulness in police-community interaction, gender bias in online communications, and "othering" in historical media representations of immigrant groups.

## Estimate of Audience Size

~50 people.

## Description of Special Requirements

- A data projector
- A computer with PowerPoint and Acrobat Reader
- Poster boards and adhesive tape
- Tables, power sockets and Internet connection, in case presenters want to give demonstrations

## Venue Preference

ACL > NAACL > EMNLP > COLING

# Deep Learning for Conversational AI

NAACL 2018 Tutorial

**Pei-Hao Su**[1], **Nikola Mrkšić**[1], **Iñigo Casanueva**[1] **Ivan Vulić**[1,2],
[1] PolyAI
[2] University of Cambridge
{eddysu, nikola, inigo, ivan}@poly-ai.com

## 1 Objectives

Spoken Dialogue Systems (SDS) have great commercial potential as they promise to revolutionise the way in which humans interact with machines. The advent of deep learning led to substantial developments in this area of NLP research, and the goal of this tutorial is to familiarise the research community with the recent advances in what some call the most difficult problem in NLP.

From a research perspective, the design of spoken dialogue systems provides a number of significant challenges, as these systems depend on: **a)** solving several difficult NLP and decision-making tasks; and **b)** combining these into a functional dialogue system pipeline. A key long-term goal of dialogue system research is to enable open-domain systems that can converse about arbitrary topics and assist humans with completing a wide range of tasks. Furthermore, such systems need to autonomously learn on-line to improve their performance and recover from errors using both signals from their environment and from implicit and explicit user feedback. While the design of such systems has traditionally been modular, domain and language-specific, advances in deep learning have alleviated many of the design problems.

The main purpose of this tutorial is to encourage dialogue research in the NLP community by providing the research background, a survey of available resources, and giving key insights to application of state-of-the-art SDS methodology into industry-scale systems. We plan to introduce researchers to the pipeline framework for modelling goal-oriented dialogue systems, which includes three key components: **1)** Language Understanding; **2)** Dialogue Management; and **3)** Language Generation. The differences between goal-oriented dialogue systems and chat-bot style conversational agents will be explained in order to show the motivation behind the design of both, with the main focus on the pipeline SDS framework. For each key component, we will define the research problem, provide a brief literature review and introduce the current state-of-the-art approaches. Complementary resources (e.g. available datasets and toolkits) will also be discussed. Finally, future work, outstanding challenges, and current industry practices will be presented. All of the presented material will be made available online for future reference.

## 2 Tutorial Overview

### 2.1 Part I: Introduction to Statistical Dialogue Systems

The modular architecture of a goal-oriented spoken dialogue system will be introduced and the range of approaches available for each component, from rule-based to (increasingly) statistical methods will be discussed. The key architectural requirements of goal-oriented spoken dialogue systems will be emphasised and the differences to chat-bot style systems will be explained. Based on this introduction, the key challenges for machine learning will be identified and the options available for moving from the current generation of limited domain systems to fully open-domain conversational agents will be presented. A particular focus will be on learning techniques which enable a system to incrementally increase its naturalness, robustness and coverage over time by interaction on-line with real users.

### 2.2 Part II: Language Understanding and Dialogue State Tracking

In this part, we will present the *language understanding* module, which is the first component of the SDS pipeline. This module takes as input the users' spoken/written utterances and converts them to an abstract



*Proceedings of NAACL-HLT 2018: Tutorial Abstracts*, pages 27–32
New Orleans, Louisiana, June 1, 2018. 

representation that the downstream dialogue management component can (learn to) operate and reason with. We plan to give an overview of: **a)** rule-based systems; **b)** conventional approaches which split the language understanding problem into Spoken Language Understanding (**SLU**) and Belief Tracking (**BT**); and **c)** the most recent models which learn to perform the two tasks jointly. In presenting these approaches, we will focus on two key challenges: **1)** mitigating the effect of automatic speech recognition (ASR) errors; and **2)** dealing with the ambiguity introduced by the linguistic variations available to users in expressing their intentions in various dialogue contexts. Finally, the impact that recent advances in representation learning have had on language understanding will be discussed: these very recent fully statistical approaches hold promise to drive progress in domain adaptation for dialogue systems, both across *different dialogue domains* and *across different languages.*

### 2.3 Part III: Dialogue Management and Reinforcement Learning

This part will focus on how the turn-taking process is managed in an SDS. The role of the dialogue manager is to map the inferred belief state into a meaningful system action, accounting for the uncertainty propagated from the upstream components. The basics of reinforcement learning (RL) will first be introduced, followed by its practical application to the dialogue management task. We will cover: **a)** tabular-based RL, which is only tractable for simplified problems; **b)** Gaussian process-based RL, which enables fast policy learning; and **c)** deep (neural network-based) RL which has the potential to eliminate the explicit need for hand-crafted feature engineering. We will also show how a dialogue policy can be trained off-line on corpora via supervised learning, and on-line with a user simulator or through direct interaction with human users using RL. When learning with human users, task success can be hard to measure and user feedback is often unreliable and difficult to obtain. To deal with this, a literature review will be covered, and especially Gaussian Process estimators will be presented which minimise the burden on users of providing explicit feedback and mitigate the problems of noisy user feedback.

### 2.4 Part IV: Response Generation and End-to-End Dialogue Modelling

In this part of the tutorial, methods of statistical language generation will be presented, which map abstract system dialogue acts back into natural language. We will first explain how Recurrent Neural Network language models can be used to generate sentences, and how a structured meaning representation such as a dialogue act can be used to condition the generation process. We will also show that attention and gating mechanisms can be used to better model internal content selection and prevent semantic repetitions, which leads to more coherent and natural responses. Next, we will frame the response generation task in a broader context by treating end-to-end dialogue modelling as a conditional response generation task. We will draw connections between this approach and other chat-bot style conversational agents, showing that explicit language grounding is crucial for goal-oriented dialogue response generation. Finally, we will address the difficulty of collecting corpora for training the SDS systems in general and the generation module in particular. We will also discuss how a pipelined Wizard-of-Oz data collection framework can be used to collect significant amounts of data at acceptably low cost.

### 2.5 Part V: SDS Systems in Conversational AI Applications and Current Challenges

The conversational interfaces hold promise to construct a fully natural way of communication between the human and the machine. In the final part of the tutorial, we will frame modern dialogue research sub-problems in the context of broader NLP research: we will outline once more recent trends in the development of modular dialogue systems, explaining how these complement the long-term goals of broader AI research. We will also discuss the current status of deploying SDS systems beyond the core academic research: we will analyse their impact and usefulness in industry-scale applications and their potential for conversational AI. We will place special emphasis on the key challenges and open questions in our pursuit of creating open-domain statistical dialogue systems across different languages.

We will conclude by listing publicly available software packages and implementations, available training datasets and evaluation protocols, and sketching future research avenues in this domain.

## 3 Structure and Summary

**Part I:** Introduction to Statistical Dialogue Systems (*30 minutes*)

- Overview of statistical dialogue systems: related work, current trends.
- Pipeline approaches vs. chat-bot style conversational agents.
- Long-term SDS goals and its relation to conversational AI.

**Part II:** Language Understanding and Dialogue State Tracking (*40 minutes*)

- Survey of approaches for performing language understanding in spoken dialogue systems.
- The impact of advances in semantic representation learning on understanding in dialogue systems.
- Fully statistical language understanding: towards open-domain SDS systems across languages.

**Part III:** Dialogue Management and Reinforcement Learning (*40 minutes*)

- Reinforcement learning approaches for managing the turn-taking dialogue task.
- Dialogue evaluation and reward estimation for practical policy learning.

**Part IV:** Response Generation and End-to-End Dialogue Modelling (*40 minutes*)

- Response generation from structured meaning representations.
- End-to-End dialogue modelling: Models, evaluations, and data collection.

**Part V:** SDS Systems in Conversational AI Applications and Current Challenges (*30 minutes*)

- Publicly available software packages and implementations, available training datasets and evaluation protocols.
- SDS systems and conversational interfaces: research vs. industry demands.
- Key challenges and open questions in the pursuit of creating open-domain statistical dialogue systems across different languages.

## 4 About the Speakers

**Pei-Hao Su** `https://eddy0613.github.io/`; email: `eddysu@poly-ai.com`

Pei-Hao (Eddy) Su is a co-founder and CTO of PolyAI, a London-based startup looking to use the latest developments in NLP to create a general machine learning platform for deploying spoken dialogue systems. He holds a PhD from the Dialogue Systems group, University of Cambridge, where he worked under the supervision of Professor Steve Young. His research interests centre on applying deep learning, reinforcement learning and Bayesian approaches to dialogue management and reward estimation, with the aim of building systems that can learn directly from human interaction. He has given several invited talks at academia and industry such as Apple, Microsoft, General Motor and DeepHack.Turing. He received the best student paper award at ACL 2016.

**Nikola Mrkšić** `mi.eng.cam.ac.uk/~nm480`; email: `nikola@poly-ai.com`

Nikola Mrkšić is a co-founder and CEO of PolyAI, a London-based startup looking to use the latest developments in NLP to create a general machine learning platform for deploying spoken dialogue systems. He holds a PhD from the Dialogue Systems group, University of Cambridge, where he worked under the supervision of Professor Steve Young. His research is focused on belief tracking in human-machine dialogue, specifically in moving towards building open-domain, cross-lingual language understanding models that are fully data-driven. He is also interested in deep learning, semantics, Bayesian nonparametrics, unsupervised and semi-supervised learning. He previously gave a tutorial on word vector space specialisation at EACL 2017, and will teach a course on the same topic at ESSLLI 2018. He also gave invited talks at the REWORK AI Personal Assistant summit and the Chatbot Summit.

**Iñigo Casanueva** `http://mi.eng.cam.ac.uk/~ic340/`; email: `inigo@poly-ai.com`
Iñigo Casanueva is a Machine Learning engineer at PolyAI, a London-based startup looking to use the latest developments in NLP to create a general machine learning platform for deploying spoken dialogue systems. He got his PhD from the University of Sheffield and later he worked as Research Assistant in the Dialogue Systems group, University of Cambridge. His main research interest focuses on increasing the scalability of machine learning based dialogue management, looking for methods to make deep learning and/or reinforcement learning applicable to real world dialogue management tasks. He has published several papers on the topic, two of them nominated to best paper award.

**Ivan Vulić** `https://sites.google.com/site/ivanvulic/`; email: `iv250@cam.ac.uk`
Ivan Vulić is a Senior Research Associate in the Language Technology Lab at the University of Cambridge. He holds a PhD from KU Leuven, obtained summa cum laude. Ivan is interested in representation learning, human language understanding, distributional, lexical, and multi-modal semantics in monolingual and multilingual contexts, and transfer learning for enabling cross-lingual NLP applications. He co-lectured a tutorial on monolingual and multilingual topic models and applications at ECIR 2013 and WSDM 2014, a tutorial on word vector space specialisation at EACL 2017, and a tutorial on cross-lingual word representations at EMNLP 2017. He will lecture a course on word vector space specialisation at ESSLLI 2018. He has given invited talks at academia and industry such as Apple Inc., University of Cambridge, UCL, University of Copenhagen, Paris-Saclay, and Bar-Ilan University.

## 5 Other Information

- Previous tutorial editions: N/A
- Audience size (estimate): 100-120
- Special requirements: None
- Acceptable venues: 1. EMNLP, 2. NAACL-HLT, 3. ACL (sorted starting with the most preferable venue)

## Selected Bibliography

Antoine Bordes and Jason Weston. 2016. Learning end-to-end goal-oriented dialog. In *Proceedings of ICLR (Conference Track)*, volume abs/1605.07683.

Paweł Budzianowski, Stefan Ultes, Pei-Hao Su, Nikola Mrkšić, Tsung-Hsien Wen, Iñigo Casanueva, Lina M. Rojas Barahona, and Milica Gasic. 2017. Sub-domain modelling for dialogue management with hierarchical reinforcement learning. In *Proceedings of SIGDIAL*, pages 86–92, August.

Nina Dethlefs, Helen F. Hastie, Heriberto Cuayáhuitl, Yanchao Yu, Verena Rieser, and Oliver Lemon. 2016. Information density and overlap in spoken dialogue. *Computer Speech & Language*, 37:82–97.

Ondřej Dušek and Filip Jurcicek. 2015. Training a natural language generator from unaligned data. In *Proceedings of ACL*, pages 451–461.

Milica Gašić, Dilek Hakkani-Tür, and Asli Çelikyilmaz. 2017a. Spoken language understanding and interaction: Machine learning for human-like conversational systems. *Computer Speech & Language*, 46:249–251.

Milica Gašić, Nikola Mrkšić, Lina Maria Rojas-Barahona, Pei-Hao Su, Stefan Ultes, David Vandyke, Tsung-Hsien Wen, and Steve J. Young. 2017b. Dialogue manager domain adaptation using gaussian process reinforcement learning. *Computer Speech & Language*, 45:552–569.

Matthew Henderson, Milica Gašić, Blaise Thomson, Pirros Tsiakoulis, Kai Yu, and Steve J. Young. 2012. Discriminative spoken language understanding using word confusion networks. In *Proceedings of IEEE SLT*, pages 176–181.

Matthew Henderson, Blaise Thomson, and Steve Young. 2013. Deep neural network approach for the Dialog State Tracking Challenge. In *Proceedings of SIGDIAL*, pages 467–471.

Matthew Henderson, Blaise Thomson, and Steve Young. 2014. Word-based dialog state tracking with recurrent neural networks. In *Proceedings of SIGDIAL*, pages 292–299.

Matthew Henderson. 2015. *Discriminative Methods for Statistical Spoken Dialogue Systems*. Ph.D. thesis, University of Cambridge.

Youngsoo Jang, Jiyeon Ham, Byung-Jun Lee, Youngjae Chang, and Kee-Eung Kim. 2016. Neural dialog state tracker for large ontologies by attention mechanism. In *IEEE SLT*, pages 531–537.

Seokhwan Kim, Luis Fernando D'Haro, Rafael E. Banchs, Jason D. Williams, Matthew Henderson, and Koichiro Yoshino. 2016. The fifth dialog state tracking challenge. In *Proceedings of IEEE SLT*, pages 511–517.

Jiwei Li, Will Monroe, Alan Ritter, Dan Jurafsky, Michel Galley, and Jianfeng Gao. 2016. Deep reinforcement learning for dialogue generation. In *Proceedings of EMNLP*, pages 1192–1202, November.

Jiwei Li, Will Monroe, Tianlin Shi, Sébastien Jean, Alan Ritter, and Dan Jurafsky. 2017. Adversarial learning for neural dialogue generation. In *Proceedings of EMNLP*, pages 2157–2169.

Bing Liu and Ian Lane. 2016. Joint online spoken language understanding and language modeling with recurrent neural networks. In *Proceedings of SIGDIAL*, pages 22–30.

Chia-Wei Liu, Ryan Lowe, Iulian Serban, Mike Noseworthy, Laurent Charlin, and Joelle Pineau. 2016. How NOT to evaluate your dialogue system: An empirical study of unsupervised evaluation metrics for dialogue response generation. In *Proceedings of EMNLP*, pages 2122–2132.

Nikola Mrkšić, Diarmuid Ó Séaghdha, Blaise Thomson, Milica Gašić, Pei-Hao Su, David Vandyke, Tsung-Hsien Wen, and Steve Young. 2015. Multi-domain dialog state tracking using recurrent neural networks. In *Proceedings of ACL*, pages 794–799.

Nikola Mrkšić, Diarmuid Ó Séaghdha, Blaise Thomson, Milica Gašić, Lina M. Rojas-Barahona, Pei-Hao Su, David Vandyke, Tsung-Hsien Wen, and Steve Young. 2016. Counter-fitting word vectors to linguistic constraints. In *Proceedings of NAACL-HLT*, pages 142–148.

Nikola Mrkšić, Diarmuid Ó Séaghdha, Tsung-Hsien Wen, Blaise Thomson, and Steve Young. 2017a. Neural Belief Tracker: Data-driven dialogue state tracking. In *Proceedings of ACL*, pages 1777–1788.

Nikola Mrkšić, Ivan Vulić, Diarmuid Ó Séaghdha, Ira Leviant, Roi Reichart, Milica Gašić, Anna Korhonen, and Steve Young. 2017b. Semantic specialization of distributional word vector spaces using monolingual and cross-lingual constraints. *Transactions of the Association for Computational Linguistics*, 5:309–324.

Julien Perez and Fei Liu. 2017. Dialog state tracking, a machine reading approach using memory network. In *Proceedings of EACL*, pages 305–314.

Verena Rieser and Oliver Lemon. 2011. Learning and evaluation of dialogue strategies for new applications: Empirical methods for optimization from small data sets. *Computational Linguistics*, 37(1):153–196.

Iulian Vlad Serban, Alessandro Sordoni, Yoshua Bengio, Aaron C. Courville, and Joelle Pineau. 2016. Building end-to-end dialogue systems using generative hierarchical neural network models. In *Proceedings of AAAI*, pages 3776–3784.

Pei-Hao Su, David Vandyke, Milica Gašić, Nikola Mrkšić, Tsung-Hsien Wen, and Steve Young. 2015. Reward shaping with recurrent neural networks for speeding up on-line policy learning in spoken dialogue systems. In *Proceedings of SIGDIAL*, pages 417–421, September.

Pei-Hao Su, Milica Gašić, Nikola Mrkšić, Lina M. Rojas Barahona, Stefan Ultes, David Vandyke, Tsung-Hsien Wen, and Steve Young. 2016. On-line active reward learning for policy optimisation in spoken dialogue systems. In *Proceedings of ACL*, pages 2431–2441.

Pei-Hao Su, Paweł Budzianowski, Stefan Ultes, Milica Gasic, and Steve Young. 2017. Sample-efficient actor-critic reinforcement learning with supervised data for dialogue management. In *Proceedings of SIGDIAL*, pages 147–157.

Blaise Thomson. 2009. *Statistical methods for spoken dialogue management.* Ph.D. thesis, University of Cambridge.

Stefan Ultes, Lina M. Rojas Barahona, Pei-Hao Su, David Vandyke, Dongho Kim, Iñigo Casanueva, Paweł Budzianowski, Nikola Mrkšić, Tsung-Hsien Wen, Milica Gašić, and Steve Young. 2017. PyDial: A multi-domain statistical dialogue system toolkit. In *Proceedings of ACL Demos*, pages 73–78.

David Vandyke, Pei-hao Su, Milica Gašić, Nikola Mrkšić, Tsung-Hsien Wen, and Steve Young. 2015. Multi-domain dialogue success classifiers for policy training. In *Proceedings of ASRU*, pages 763–770.

Oriol Vinyals and Quoc V. Le. 2015. A neural conversational model. *CoRR*, abs/1506.05869.

Miroslav Vodolán, Rudolf Kadlec, and Jan Kleindienst. 2017. Hybrid dialog state tracker with ASR features. In *Proceedings of EACL*, pages 205–210.

Ivan Vulić, Nikola Mrkšić, Roi Reichart, Diarmuid Ó Séaghdha, Steve Young, and Anna Korhonen. 2017. Morph-fitting: Fine-tuning word vector spaces with simple language-specific rules. In *Proceedings of ACL*, pages 56–68.

Zhuoran Wang, Tsung-Hsien Wen, Pei-Hao Su, and Yannis Stylianou. 2015. Learning domain-independent dialogue policies via ontology parameterisation. In *Proceedings of SIGDIAL*, pages 412–416.

Joseph Weizenbaum. 1966. ELIZA - A computer program for the study of natural language communication between man and machine. *Communications of the ACM*, 9(1):36–45.

Tsung-Hsien Wen, Milica Gašić, Dongho Kim, Nikola Mrkšić, Pei-Hao Su, David Vandyke, and Steve Young. 2015a. Stochastic language generation in dialogue using recurrent neural networks with convolutional sentence reranking. In *Proceedings of SIGDIAL*, pages 275–284.

Tsung-Hsien Wen, Milica Gašić, Nikola Mrkšić, Pei-Hao Su, David Vandyke, and Steve Young. 2015b. Semantically conditioned LSTM-based natural language generation for spoken dialogue systems. In *Proceedings of EMNLP*, pages 1711–1721.

Tsung-Hsien Wen, Milica Gašić, Nikola Mrkšić, Lina M. Rojas-Barahona, Pei-Hao Su, David Vandyke, and Steve Young. 2016. Multi-domain neural network language generation for spoken dialogue systems. In *Proceedings of NAACL-HLT*, pages 120–129.

Tsung-Hsien Wen, Yishu Miao, Phil Blunsom, and Steve J. Young. 2017a. Latent intention dialogue models. In *Proceedings of ICML*, pages 3732–3741.

Tsung-Hsien Wen, David Vandyke, Nikola Mrkšić, Milica Gašić, Lina M. Rojas Barahona, Pei-Hao Su, Stefan Ultes, and Steve Young. 2017b. A network-based end-to-end trainable task-oriented dialogue system. In *Proceedings of EACL*, pages 438–449.

Jason Williams, Antoine Raux, and Matthew Henderson. 2016. The dialog state tracking challenge series: A review. *Dialogue&Discourse*, 7(3):4–33.

Jason Williams. 2013. Multi-domain learning and generalization in dialog state tracking. In *Proceedings of SIGDIAL*, pages 433–441.

Steve Young, Milica Gašić, Blaise Thomson, and Jason D. Williams. 2013. POMDP-Based statistical spoken dialog systems: A review. *Proceedings of the IEEE*, 101(5):1160–1179.

Steve Young. 2010a. Cognitive User Interfaces. *IEEE Signal Processing Magazine*.

Steve Young. 2010b. Still talking to machines (cognitively speaking). In *Proceedings of INTERSPEECH*, pages 1–10.

# Author Index

**Association for Computational Linguistics**
209 N. Eighth Street
Stroudsburg, Pennsylvania 18360

CURRAN ASSOCIATES INC.
proceedings.com

ISBN 978-1-5108-6351-4

9 781510 863514